I0151442

Words and Bones

poems by

LB Sedlacek

Finishing Line Press
Georgetown, Kentucky

Words and Bones

ACKNOWLEDGMENTS

"Fortune Cookie Poem #31" was originally published in *Bindweed Magazine*
"Visible Thing" was originally published in *Dash Literary Journal*
"How to Sculpt" was originally published in *Poetry Quarterly*
"Whispered Silence" was originally published in *ArtMag*
"Flying Order" was originally published in *Random Sample Review*
"Edge Code" was originally published in *Sand Journal*
"About a Waitress" was originally published in *The Faircloth Review*
"The Bed Dance" was originally published in *Poetic Diversity*
"Bruising History" was originally published in *Sick Lit Magazine*
"Carolina Beach Arcade" was originally published in *Bindweed Magazine*
"Up at the Ski Lift" was originally published as part of *Poetry Super
    Highway*'s Poet of the Week

Publisher: Leah Maines
Editor: Christen Kincaid
Cover Art: Ry Sedlacek
Author Photo: Ry Sedlacek
Cover Design: Elizabeth Maines McCleavy

Printed in the USA on acid-free paper.
Order online: www.finishinglinepress.com
            also available on amazon.com

Author inquiries and mail orders:
Finishing Line Press
P. O. Box 1626
Georgetown, Kentucky 40324
U. S. A.

Table of Contents

Words and Bones

Wadded up note in pocket
been in there since Spring
all through the summer and some
into Winter a note written
on scrap paper wadded up
three things written on it
lanyard, tissues and sympathy cards
not exactly in that order
this wadded up note won't
be thrown in the trash
it will be kept with
other pieces of scrap paper
to store someone's forgotten words

We want souvenirs

By the dugout
Near first base
Kids of all
Ages stream up
And down the
Bleachers with hope
Filled eyes and
Empty gloves begging
For a memory
To take home

Clearance

Clearance for weather central.
Checking maps and storms
behind enemy lines. Moved
clearance to top secret.
Checking codes and facts
keeping the enemy behind.
Clearance for medical leave.
Checking in the uniform
hiding behind fan mail.
Clearance for civilian life.
Checking and correcting mistakes
always from behind somewhere.

Clearance in everything wrong.

Small

Sometimes heroes
heroines
come in
small
sizes with
big
hearts of
bravery
laughter and
love
they don't
need
capes or
special
powers to
reach
us our
hearts
full of
their
life, light
and
new beginnings
where
one size
fits
all.

Fortune Cookie Poem #31

You will receive
some high prize
or reward.

You are patient and carefree.

Drink to your health.

Wish you
happiness.

You will inherit some
money or a
small piece of land.

You will receive
some of nothing
or none.

Fortify

Solitary fence
incomplete
only one
panel
solitary good
for
hanging hoses
kicking
mud off
shoes
solitary games
of
basketball
chain link
fence
piece without
partners
solitary surprisingly
it
doesn't look
unusual
simply functional
otherwise
solitary removal

Mixture

Dandelion greens, parsley, burdock
purslane and lamb's quarters
are full of iron,
calcium, vitamin A, vitamin C.
These greens frequently are
found in old recipes
for making tonic waters.
To sip one all
you'll need is a
blender. Enjoy on a
beach or private island.
Maybe while cooling it
sliding down water slides.
It invigorates the body.
It restores the health.

Unbound

Four chairs
Brown color
Front yard
Facing nothing
Empty row

Four chairs
Brown color
Side street
Facing traffic
Empty house

Visible Thing

The old jeans
factory
eaten alive

by kudzu for
some
time hummed

drummed along
spitting
out pants

of different hues.
The
kids playing

by the creek
could
always tell

the color of
the
dye that

day by looking
at
the water.

Repay

Discarded receipts scattered
to the floor
each with a
story and a
need for cash
in a restaurant
that only takes
cash or checks
food served family
style all you
can eat including
dessert two choices
tonight more than
enough and more
than enough must
have been in
the ATM to
cover all the
payers that usually
pay in plastic

Melted Crayons

The plastic surgery of a tomato
may be necessary if your plants
are healthy but the flowers fall
off prematurely. The tomato could have
blossom drop which can be caused
by high temperatures (85° F or 75° F)
by low temperatures (below 55° nights)
excess nitrogen
high humidity
low humidity.

The plastic surgery of a tomato
may look good on you at first
if you are healthy and your
face is full. You could still
experience drop off sometimes caused by
age, lack of elasticity and volume
in your skin, or genetics
sun exposure
facial expressions
thinning skin

drop off.

Scenes from a Car Line

Every day I sit in the car line
mostly invisible
and some days I see
someone I know
but I often don't choose
to speak preferring invisibility

Most days I read poetry
or about poetry
sometimes fiction
and some days I nap
but it's too hard with the
heat or the rain
or the whirr and roar
of someone else's car

There is no need for an
electronic device
sometimes newspapers or magazines
fill the void and most
anything will do
business, entertainment, science

Every day in the car line
there's something new
yellow and black birds today
a new tree branch tomorrow
a fallen birdhouse yesterday
still that doesn't preclude
paying attention and being ready
when the line finally starts to move.

How to Sculpt

Scraps of paper
newspapers torn in
pieces or magazine
articles ripped out
billboard signs seen
from the highways
a phrase here
a line from
a movie or
a TV show
a memory from
the past or
the quick short
term present fleeting
even as these
words these scraps
are stuck together
pasted by a
pencil a pen
a computer keyboard
maybe a smart
phone all meeting
the final task
the letter molding
the word gluing
the hands shaping
sentences, every one.

Fence Surfing

Profile face
craggy boulders
in the right light
hands clenched
wire fence
watching a baseball game
he turns
grabs drinks
stuffs them into pockets
his chairs
packed up
he's ready to leave
rainy field
and me
behind

umex acetosa

Juice from the sorrel plant
removes rust, mold and ink
stains from linen, silver and
wicker. It's a handy herb.

HIT (Hibernation Induction Trigger)

A substance
present
in the
blood
of bears
and
other animals
where
changes in
daylight
and
in temperature
trigger
its action
inducing
animal hibernation
even
when it's
not
winter, not
time
not even
the
full
wolf moon
or
time for
a
fresh edition
of
nature's news.

The Fifth

Take the fifth
doesn't refer to
the constitution but
to a Fifth
Avenue a car
the dream of
splashed in bright
colors painted on
a license plate
pink yellow blue
the first one
that special car
which when traded
in is always
remembered and missed.

Whispered Silence

He moved his lips this morning.
There was no sound, but I'd
turned it down, but when I
turned it up all I could hear
was the hum of the signal.
It was faded and blocked by the trees
and those eyesore cell phone
towers that never send a signal
when you need it. I whacked the
TV but that didn't help. My
eyes seized on a caption that
explained why there was no
sound. I took my cell phone
and whacked it on the counter.
I dropped it in the sink to see
if it would float. I dropped
one in a toilet two years
ago and it sank like my
hand did when I spotted a
fish and tried to grab it.
His lips keep moving and I
watch them transfixed. I look
up "transmogrification" in
the dictionary and think there
are more words than I could
ever imagine that start with
"ex." I stare at his mouth,
his beard, his curly black
and white hair and realize
that I heard every word.

Flying Order

Insects of the order Diptera
are true flies
possessing a single pair of wings
on the mesothorax
plus a pair of halteres
(derived from the hind wings)
also on the mesothorax.

Possession of a single pair of wings
distinguishes a true fly
from other insects
with "fly" in their name.
Well adapted for aerial movement
short and streamlined bodies
a mobile head with eyes
short antennae
to reduce drag while flying.

One floating in an iced coffee
One buzzing in the office
One flying in a restaurant
One interrupting a president

Diptera is a large order
estimated at over 240,000 species.

Still, why all this fuss about flies?
They only consume liquid food.

Turf

This unfinished quilt
these trembling hands
left to stitch
memories and legacies
owed together into
a finished piece
of white, green
red and yellow
the cloth stretched
one panel complete
to be sewn
not by machines
but by hand
so many machines
nine in all
that do different
things and do
different tasks all
of them idle
now with no
projects left except
the memory quilt
sewn by hand
in the basement
room with the
sewing machines sitting
unused and vacant.

Edge Code

Numbered coding on the edge of film,
work prints, final cuts, rushes,
those numbers could be made
into something more -- predictions
of earthquakes, hurricanes, meteors,
or maybe leave a numerical
puzzle in plain sight, mash notes
for a mathematician matching
visual to sound putting things into
slow motion, that rush feeling felt
when meeting someone new with
the potential to be more than a
first sighting off a ship, from a
lighthouse or from wherever what's
wanted is swimming deep that day.

Ease

High grass
fallen markers
forgotten cemetery
in weeds
left behind
from suicide
no family
members left
to tend
the graves.

Terra Firma Lane

Parking on grass
not past the tree
leaves in piles
old men telling stories
Christmas tree lightings
Train cabooses and windmills
and when this old school was once
a boarding school

we sit on uneven
benches covered up
with paint and read
posters for basketball
games years in the
past and folks
talk and eat funnel cake or cotton
candy while they wait

for the competition
to end and the
old man says
it's good they found
another use for
the school but the
buildings are run down and in need
of repair and

he's right because the
clock tower's four
faces are all set
to different times
6pm, 4pm, 12 noon
and 1 o'clock and there's no one left
to fix it.

About a Waitress

Tonight I had ivory cheesecake with
a candle on top
a birthday celebration
three weeks late.

The invitation is crisp and ivory
with chocolate letters,
leading to a chapel.
The events familiar, but
a surprise to some.

It's always about a waitress
or someone young that prefers
power to looks, money to physique.
I don't think this is what any
of the fairy tales had in mind:
"Hey Princess go marry someone
old enough to be your Father."

I eat my cheesecake with a spoon.
I blow out the candle after
the waitress takes my order just
so a little smoke gets in her eyes.

The Bed Dance

At night we toss and tumble, laundry
travels slick on silk sheets. My
nose crinkles at the wave of leaves
flip flopping on porpoise backs, shiny
as the morning dew
or water beads
on tea cups overflowing with hangover
stew, insomniac soup. Your eyes
are rough on my skin, the mattress
groans as I flip on a flashlight
in search of a drink of water
to wash the salt out of my hair.

Bruising History

Each window had a candle
lit every day all day
a burning bright white light
the man living there said
his wife liked the lights
something to do with her
history
their neighbor across the street
his house had no candles
it was overgrown with vines
he was a friendly man
giving away apples or tomatoes
until his son murdered his
history
the candles stayed lit awhile
soon the windows were dark
neighbors house disappeared in vines
soon leveled to the ground
and for sale signs staked
the houses now with no
history

Carolina Beach Arcade

The first time I learned about
divorce we were at the beach.
It was my cousin's parents. He didn't
understand it at first. Then he
was angry and bitter.

The arcade and the amusement
park by the beach, one in Carolina,
had bumper cars, a Ferris wheel,
Octopus, Bobsled, a game room
and a busy boardwalk.

He'd disappear on the boardwalk and
wouldn't ride the rides because he
said he had no money for tickets.
I gave him some of mine but he
didn't ride with me.

We went home. We went separate ways.
His father moved out. He stayed with
his mother. He's friends with his father
now some twenty years later and married
with his own kids.

The amusement park, the arcade, it still
sits there by the ocean. It's mostly known
now for its donut and taffy shops. Last time
I went I wasn't alone. We didn't ride the
rides or play games.

We just walked on the boardwalk and left.

Up at the Ski Lift

Our sunglasses are wrapped
to our heads
shiny and glowing underneath
goggles squeezed
tight on toboggans
our gloves thick wrapped
tight to our fingers
barely gripping the rope
pulling the snowboard
up to the counter to pay.

5200 feet, a high elevation,
but with Spring too early and
manmade snow like a thin
ribbon of caulk the bright
yellow snowboard, round
and cranky, is our best
option. And, note: will
keep us wrapped tight
around a tree, or worse.

We zip up our jackets
and jump!

The Last Great American Pin-Up

Two acrobats examining the
floor to ceiling stained glass
window some sort of scene
from a park and they run
their hands and their fingers
over the colors the gold
the yellow the green the blue
the picture nearly as effective
as the calendar pin-up girls
from the 40's and the 50's
the last one, Jewel Flowers,
posed for almost 20 years
for artist Rolf Armstrong, the
father of the American Pin-Up
his pictures painted in red
and yellow and green and gold
and pink and blue
models drawn by illustrators
their silhouettes reproduced
on the front of bombers and other
planes in World War II
pin-up girls whose images
were known to millions of Americans.

Custom Color Regrets

Plastic boxes can't prevent the
musty smell
like breathing in a new
pair of leather shoes.
The old comic books were a bargain
at 30 cents
worth more in mint condition
like leather sole stitching sewn by hand
the pages tied together in hand drawn color
the shoe patterns sketched and cut by hand
the covers filled with bright characters
the soles stamped with a one of a kind design.
How easy it is to store the old comic books
sealing them up in plastic boxes
stuffed under bags and boxes in the closet
while the shoes get worn, repaired
worn again then tossed or
maybe given away.

Parlor Soldiers

The candles are the first clue
spread out in scattered locations
like soldiers but with a sweet
honeysuckle smell. There is one
strategically placed on the countertop –
Formica blood red – at odds with the
dark wood paneling, the light beige
carpet. Everything has its place –
bills and important papers in a side drawer
and all the doors closed, the ones that
lead to other rooms hiding muffled
sounds like prisoners of war except
this isn't a battle or if it is
I'm prepared to lose.

Parlor Soldiers, Part 2

At our family parties
we would shoot fireworks
in the backyard with
a hose at the
ready in case of
fire and later the
grown-ups would go
inside to talk or
dance or sip wine
from plastic cups or
rubble on tiny square
sandwiches while the kids
stayed outside in the
dark with a long
gray and red flashlight
round circle like a
magnifying glass in the
end and play Spotlight
calling out the word
incessantly shining the light
in the trees or
the bushes underneath the
windows or in the
woods searching for the
other players something like
hide and seek except
you never knew if
you might step on
a stray firework or
not.

LB Sedlacek is a poet, author, editor, poem critic and publisher. She has had poetry and short fiction published in numerous journals and zines. Her poetry and short fiction have won several awards. She co-hosted *ESC! Magazine's* podcast for the small press, "Coffee House to Go" with Michael Potter. She also served as a Poetry Editor for *ESC! Magazine.* She is the Publisher of *The Poetry Market Ezine* a poetry resource newsletter just for poets.

She holds a BA in Business from Lenoir-Rhyne University and an MA in Communications and Theatre from Wake Forest University. She lives in North Carolina with her family and their hyperactive dog! In her free time, she enjoys reading, swimming, and volunteering for her local humane society.

Her website is www.lbsedlacek.com Find her on Facebook @ lbsedlacekpoet or Instagram @poetryinla